John F. Foard

North America and Africa

Their past, present and future

John F. Foard

North America and Africa
Their past, present and future

ISBN/EAN: 9783744755139

Printed in Europe, USA, Canada, Australia, Japan

Cover: Foto ©ninafisch / pixelio.de

More available books at **www.hansebooks.com**

NORTH AMERICA AND AFRICA:

THEIR

PAST, PRESENT AND FUTURE.

BY

JOHN F. FOARD, M. D.,

EUPEPTIC SPRINGS, IREDELL COUNTY, N. C., MAY 20, 1875,

Second Edition, November 1, 1876.

A CENTENNIAL COMPROMISE. NORTH CAROLINA WAS
FIRST TO DECLARE OUR INDEPENDENCE. LET
HER BE FIRST TO OFFER A COMPROMISE
OF OUR CIVIL TROUBLES.

DEDICATED TO THE SUFFERING POOR OF AMERICA AND AFRICA.

RALEIGH:

JOHN NICHOLS, BOOK AND JOB PRINTER.

1877.

PREFACE TO FIRST EDITION.

In offering this little book to the public, the writer begs leave to say it is written in the interest of humanity. He is no politician; never an office-holder, either civil or military, under any government. For thirty years a hard worker in all the financial and benevolent enterprises in his reach; has been a great sufferer in health, spirits and fortune, from the results of the late war, which he had no hand in creating, no power to avert, nor pleasure in its continuance; but always viewed it as a great calamity which wise statesmen ought to have prevented; and, failing to do so, believes the private, hard working citizens should no longer suffer for the error of others, but that after four years of devastating war and ten years of hardships, anxiety and distress, we should now be relieved and permitted to spend the remnant of our days in the enjoyment of comfort, peace and prosperity.

THE AUTHOR.

May 20, 1875.

PREFACE TO SECOND EDITION.

Being solicited by friends to amplify this humble volume so as to bring out more facts in relation to these great countries, and to give additional evidences of the great importance of developing them, is the apology offered for issuing a second edition of North America and Africa, and in order to give the reader the benefit of the opinions of others, better acquainted with the subjects discussed, the author will draw on the writings of learned clergymen and statesmen, who have given colonization much attention, hoping thereby to enlist the masses of both races in every section of the country, in a compromise, which is offered in the spirit of Christianity and philanthrophy, and will accomplish, if adopted, much good for both countries and both races. And as the first edition was written in a few hours ride of the spot where our independence was first declared, and on the Centennial day of said event, so the second edition fittingly appears in the great Centennial year of our national history.

THE AUTHOR.

November 1, 1876.

NORTH AMERICA AND AFRICA.

CHAPTER I

These two grand divisions of the Eastern and Western Hemispheres, with their varieties of climate, valuable products, and hundreds of millions of human beings must, in due time, become most important fields of operation, under God, in the civilization and evangelization of the world. The one, situated north of the equator, between the Atlantic and Pacific Oceans, and extending towards the North Pole, containing extensive ranges of mountains, expansive lakes, numerous rivers, and necessarily a cold country, is adapted to and is destined to be occupied by the Anglo-Saxon or white race, because of their superior energy, thrift, power of endurance, and indomitable will to conquer; and this important part of the Western Hemisphere is rapidly being occupied, cultivated and improved by this race, though other races have been in possession or introduced from time to time. Thus we see in about three hundred years from the time this race of people placed foot upon this continent, millions of acres of forest have been cleared, ready for the ploughshare of the husbandman, hundreds of cities been built, numerous lakes and rivers navigated, thousands of miles of railroads and telegraph lines put in successful operation; schools, colleges and universities established in every section; churches and benevolent societies scattered all over this vast territory. Life, energy and progress are seen and felt in all these institutions and instruments. In one hundred years a great government has been formed on this continent by this

people, extending from the St. Lawrence to the Rio Grande ;
for which the history of the world affords no parallel ; a
matter of astonishment to ourselves and the world; and
we, its occupants, can only look up and exclaim, " What
hath God wrought " in one day and country ?

Considering all the circumstances which have attended
us, though the world is six thousand years old, there has
been more accomplished in a century by our government
and people, some of whose ancestors were slaves less than
three thousand years ago, and who fled from persecution
in search of rest and peace, than any people in any ten
centuries of the world's history. How is all this to be
accounted for ? Not by human wisdom or strength alone.
For centuries ago man was learned in the arts and sciences
to a wonderful extent, but depreciated in both until he
well nigh lost all that he ever possessed. Then we must
look to a higher and purer source for light to enable us to
solve this problem. God's providence is in all this.

To continue to develop the resources of America and
improve the condition of our government should be the
desire of every citizen, and to elevate the condition of man
everywhere is the duty of all who can write or speak.

While much has been done, much more must be done to
make North America what it is capable of being made.
The late war between the States destroyed for a time our
labor, commerce and trade, creating a fictitious value on
every article of luxury and necessity, while it lasted, and
since, depressed the prices of our products to a wonderful degree below remunerative prices, and impoverished so
many thousands of our people who were once able to buy
foreign goods, that a great financial panic has come upon
us. Foreign goods have been reshipped whence they came
by importers, or sold at ruinous prices ; domestic goods are
dragging on the market ; manufacturers and dealers are
making smaller sales and less profits than formerly ; cotton

and other mills are running on half time; the wages of operatives and laborers greatly reduced or totally suspended; Western horses, mules, bacon and grain are selling more slowly and cheaply than for many years; Southern cotton, tobacco and other products are going for less than the cost of their production, and money, though plenty, more difficult to obtain than ever before.

To readjust matters to a state of equilibrium should be the aim of every statesman and citizen in our government, that universal peace be established, confidence and good-will be restored and remunerative employment be given to the people. How is all this to be done? Let the general government deal with all her citizens alike. If all are citizens, let all share equally the privileges as well as the burdens, to sustain the government; if all pay taxes, let all come in for a fair distribution of public favors; we are all of one family and should enjoy equal rights in a government made for us all.

The civil war was a sectional strife for sectional and individual rights under a constitution made by the blood and sufferings of our forefathers and for us all, and was the common heritage of us all. And now, as we are reconstructed, let us all enjoy equal rights and privileges under the government.

The Union men, as they were called, of the South as well as the North, who took an oath of loyalty, have been paid for their property destroyed for them on land and sea by the armies and navies of both sides; let all others of our citizens be treated in the same way. Some of the Union soldiers have been pensioned; let Southern soldiers who are living and the families of those who are dead, be remunerated for their lost time, lives and fortunes, as it was a sectional or civil strife, and many of them were forced into service and others persuaded to oppose a sectional war. Let restitution be made to all as far as possible, for it was

a fratricidal, civil strife, began for emancipation, and
resisted for individual rights.

Let our present internal revenue system be greatly modi-
fied or repealed; take all direct tax off the people and col-
lect revenue for the payment of the present and increased
national debt by port duties and the sale of public lands, as
before the war. Consolidate the present national debt with
the amount necessary to compensate all our people of every
section, at least, in part, for all their losses and services in-
cident upon the war, which ruined both sections and all
classes, by issuing new bonds, which may be paid to the
people, and take up the outstanding bonds, the interest to
be paid annually and the principal in such installments in
the future, as a growing and prosperous nation can pay
without direct taxation. The sudden and forcible emancipation of the slaves of the South, greatly damaged both
races in the South and the laboring whites of the North
and West, and the results are now being felt in all the
States; and the alienation between the white and the colored people of the South, produced by the bad advice of
adventurers from abroad, is now so great as to demand a
final separation of the two races ; such is the ill feeling now
entertained by the colored people toward their former
owners and best friends, as to make it impossible for the two
races to continue to live together in unity; as a proof of
which it is only necessary to look in our files of old papers,
court records, jails and penitentiaries, and see how the crimes
of larceny, rape, incendiarism and murder have multiplied
since the war; as many as twenty colored men have gone
from a single court to the State prison at one time, and
though our prisons are all overflowing and the convicts are
put on public works by the thousand, those crimes are on
the increase. Where is the end of all this ? And what is
the remedy ? Colonization is the only human remedy for
these and other existing evils. Aid from the general gov-

ernment is absolutely necessary to secure this act of justice and humanity.

––––––––––––

CHAPTER II.

Since the first act of disobedience on the part of man, and his consequent fall from his original state of purity and likeness of his Creator, down through the entire history of the world, he has, by voluntary acts of transgression, alienated himself from his God and brought temporal and eternal destruction upon his race. And since the great act of rebellion in building the Tower of Babel, the race has been divided into different races of different languages, colors, habits and customs, each occupying respective parts of the earth most suitable to his condition. Thus we see the white man occupying the most northern and colder countries, while the colored man has occupied the southern and warmer parts of the earth. Africa is near and south of the equator, a vast, tropical country, with millions of acres of the most fertile and easily worked level land along the coast, and salubrious mountain country, with minerals in the interior; from time immemorial the home of the negro race, a country made for and peculiarly adapted to the condition, nature and habits of that people. The wisdom and providence of God may be seen in all these divisions of the race of man, and his location, climate and products of the different countries for his habitation and culture. For thousands of years Africa has been the home of the unenlightened, indolent and savage tribes of people, who were constantly warring with each other and selling their captives into slavery; and until the great Dr. Livingston explored the country and learned the habits of its occupants, the world was comparatively ignorant of both

2

land and population. Thirty-three years of incessant labor, privation and hardships, thousands of dollars, and the life of that noble, learned, philanthropic, Christian man, were expended that the world might learn the geography, capabilities, extent and value of that country, and the wants of the people.

Both the Old and New Testament abound in passages indicating the redemption of Africa and her children. And to the intelligent Christian there are visible signs of a speedy approach of the great and eventful day, when no only Africa shall be redeemed, but when the world shall be converted into a second Eden and man restored to his former state of purity and favor in the eyes of his Creator. However, before this can be done, the gospel must be carried to all nations and peoples, and Africa and her children will share in this important work. "The wolf also shall dwell with the lamb, and the leopard shall lie down with the kid, and the calf and the young lion and the fatling together, and a little child shall lead them, and the cow and the bear shall feed; and their young ones shall lie down together, and the lion shall eat straw like the ox. And the sucking child shall play on the hole of the asp, and the weaned child shall put his hand on the cockatrice's den. They shall not hurt nor destroy in all My holy mountain, for the earth shall be full of the knowledge of the Lord as the waters cover the sea."—Isaiah XI: 6-9. "The wilderness and solitary places shall be glad for them, and the desert shall rejoice and blossom as the rose."—Isaiah XXXV: 1. The government of the United States of America and her people are doubtless to be instruments in the hands of God employed to redeem Africa; her two hundred millions of benighted people must be enlightened by the efforts of this Christian nation, so full of resources and enterprise. England has explored Africa, and now it is left to America to cultivate it, and the United States government and people should be the principal instruments in the civilization and Christianization of that people. Many of our earliest and most able divines and statesmen were of this opinion. Rev. Robert Finly, D. D., Bishop Bascome, the Lees, Hons. Henry Clay, Webster, Everett, Randolph, Bushrod Washington and others, North and South, believed this, and labored for it in the establishment of the American Colonization Society and its auxiliaries, and the liberal expenditure of their time and money, the fruits of which may be seen in the establishment of the republic of Liberia, on the western coast of Africa—a republic modeled after ours, and which has been in existence more than half a century, and is doing much to open up the "regions beyond," preparatory for a more continued and extensive effort on the part of our nation and people. Thus a Christian nation has been formed in that far off heathen land, has existed for fifty-nine years, been managed by a people recently in bondage, and is now ready to receive the four millions of recently emancipated slaves of America. England has formed a colony, Sierra Leone, which is older than Liberia, and north of it on the same coast, and is also a success.

These colonies are worked in the interest of Christianity and civilization, and are growing rapidly and extending their power and influence for good far into the interior, and doubtless will do much towards giving "more light" and truth to their benighted brethren. But they need help! When we view the enormous task to be performed, and the comparatively small results accomplished, some will conclude that the work "can never be done." Had Columbus listened to the Solomons of his day, America might now be the home and hunting ground of the wild Indian, instead of the great and growing, influential, Christian nation that she is; and if Fulton had not persevered in his ideas of steam navigation, contrary to the opinions of the vast

majority of the intelligent people of England and America,
these grand and glorious countries might to-day be traversed by horse-power and the diminutive stage coach, instead of the magnificent steamers which now plough their
waters, and the convenient and luxurious palace cars that
fly along their numerous railways. Columbus and Fulton
are dead, but their works live to give honor to their memo-
ries and glory to God. The Christian men who formed the
Colonization Societies in Europe and America and the Republic in Africa, most of them are dead, but their efforts
still live to bless the world. The colonies in Africa have
done well to live through the perils of infancy and youth.
Now they need help to enable them to enter successfully
into a state of maturity and usefulness ; to open roads back
into the interior, to navigate rivers, subdue the forests, open
mines of gold and other minerals, reclaim marshes, ascend
and cultivate mountains, and bind together, in one homo-
geneous mass, the many barbarous and warlike tribes of
their fatherland; teach them their language, civilization
and religion. To do this will require centuries unless aid
is afforded them. Where is that aid to come from ? The
poverty of the Southern States, produced by the results of
the late war, render our people unable to do much in this
great work; and the terrific panic, which has swept over
this entire country, was felt in Europe, is still being felt in
both countries, and was the natural result of our losses, is
preventing people of the North and West from aiding in
colonizing the American people of color in Africa. Then
it is seen that the general government is alone able to
extend the necessary aid for the removal of the colored
people. They were brought here by the will and sanction
of the parent government in Colonial times; and also since
we have been a separate government, and set at liberty by
governmental authority at great cost, and now, for the
benefit of both races here and elsewhere, they should be

assisted to return. They are too poor to go unaided, and the white people are unable or unwilling to aid them, and the work of colonization must languish, as it is doing, or receive government assistance.

These people have been here in a "state of pupilage," and are now ready to go hence on a great mission of mercy and usefulness. Shall they go? Pharaoh may say, No; but God will say, Go! Our politicians may want their votes, planters their labor and merchants their trade, but all these can be replaced by foreign population from the North and the overcrowded sections of Europe, and the vast cleared fields of the South may be converted into grazing lands for herds of cattle and sheep, or sold in small lots to thrifty immigrants, who will come and bring capital and skilled labor, and the votes, labor and trade of the colored people will be needed in Africa.

The local attachment of these people is urged by some as a reason why they will not emigrate, and, consequently, "colonization is impracticable" with them. This reason is to be considered worthless when we remember that almost all of them have been moving from place to place, county to county, and State to State since they were emancipated. Open the way for their exodus; show them the advantages to be derived by them and their posterity; give them free transportation and homes and a year's support after arriving in Africa, and it will require all the idle ships in the world, and more, to carry them as fast as they will apply for passage. But if they, or any of them, prefer to remain in this country, let a fund or a part of said fund be set aside for the education of their children. The condition of those who would remain here would be improved by this act. Thousands are now applying to the officers of the different Colonization Societies for transportation, and are refused for want of funds to send them. The necessary aid may be given by the Congress of the United States without injury or damage to *any* of our remaining population, in fact will benefit all classes by appropriating enough, say sixteen hundred millions dollars, which was about two-thirds of their value in 1860, in addition to enough to pay all white soldiers, who were in the war on both sides, a reasonable pension, and say two-thirds of the real value of all the property lost by citizens of both sections in the conflict, in bonds, bearing three per cent. interest per annum, and maturing at intervals of five or ten years during the next century, give half of the amount paid for the slaves in 1860, say eight hundred millions of dollars, in bonds, to the officers of the American Colonization Society, to be used in sending *all of the colored people,* now in the United States, and their posterity, who may *be willing* to go and provide homes and a year's support for them after arriving in Africa. An act of this kind is due the Southern people of both races, for the reasons that we were in nowise responsible for the introduction of domestic slavery, it being in existence from the days of Abraham, and perpetuated by the nations of the earth ; was introduced into this country by England, for the *expressed* purpose of "creating revenue," contrary to the protestations of the Southern Colonies ; was recognized by the Constitution of the United States ; transferred, by sale, from the Northern to the Southern States, and formed the great body of wealth of these States ; was the bone of contention that produced the war, which emancipated them, and destroyed so many lives and much property for us, and brought ruin upon the Southern people, and was the cause of the greatest panic ever felt by our people ; for it was impossible to ruin us without injuring the entire civilized world, as the Southern States were producers for the world. The people, the masses, neither North or South, East or West, were responsible for the war. Politicians, who were clamorous for office, paid lecturers and writers, who filled their pockets with European gold, fanned the flame of abolitionism and disunion in order to put the cheap products of slave labor out of the way of the great monopoly of the world, the East India Company, which spent millions of dollars in paying writers and lecturers, in order that slavery in the West Indies and the United States might be abolished, not for the love of the poor negro, but for the accumulation of wealth, by lessening the products of these countries, which would enhance the value of their own.

As there are exceptions to all rules, of course many philanthropists labored, free of charge, for their manumission, but did so in a constitutional way. Emancipation was the result of a war forced upon the South in violation of the Constitution of the United States, and our people made to acquiesce under duress vile, which is regarded by all nations as unconstitutional and not magnanimous. And the laws of justice and equity, as well as interest to the public good, would suggest that the ruined South should be *reinstated* by the general. government, at least to some extent; when, in doing so, financial relief, universal prosperity and good-will would be the results. And as this is the Centennial of American Independence, let us have a compromise, by the voice of the people of the entire nation, which will restore. our former prosperity as a nation, and reunite us in the bonds of fraternal unity, never to be again severed by sectional strife. England paid her subjects for their slaves freed for them, and also paid our people for much of the property destroyed on the high seas during the late war.

Spain, though oppressed by a heavy national debt, and disturbed by internal strife, is about to pay for the slaves liberated in Porto Rico. Will not the United States be as just as those governments? Is our government not as able to indemnify her ruined people as those are? This act of justice and magnanimity, as it would be, if passed, would not only give timely aid to the colored people and their former

owners, which is greatly needed by both parties, as well
as all others who would receive direct compensation, but
would, by reflex action, benefit and improve the condition
of *all* persons in this and other countries with whom we
trade, by putting more money in circulation, enhancing the
value of property, increasing the demand for labor and re-
viving commerce and trade everywhere; Northern manufacturing establishments need no longer run on half time
or be closed, but resume full time and full pay; Western
stock and grain bring better prices; Southern labor would
then pay to produce our products and build new enterprises.
When three-fifths of the entire property of the Southern
States, the producing portion of the nation, was destroyed
by a fearful and bloody war of four years duration, say
nothing of the loss of life of the best of our population,
who fell in the conflict, the shock was felt in every country
in the civilized world, and must continue to be felt until
restitution is made, which would bring a corresponding tide
of peace and prosperity to *us* and *all* who deal with us;
this proposition is established by the laws of political
economy and the observation of every thinking mind; for
if a firm or individual fail for a large amount, the whole
community will feel, to some extent, the injurious effects
of that failure; and on the other hand, if some enterprising
man of wealth move into a country and use his wealth in
erecting factories and other improvements which will give
employment to the people and create new markets for the'r
products, all must feel the beneficial effects of the scattering
of his money.

Restitution is one of God's laws, and should be observed
by governments as well as individuals. Retributive justice
overtakes nations and communities as well as individuals,
when they disregard the laws of restitution. "Whatsoever
ye mete it shall be measured to you again." Is not this
law, or the violation of it, producing a harvest of want and

misery in our Northern manufacturing communities at this
time? What has stopped so many mills, reduced rents,
cut down wages, and is producing so much distress at the
North? Why is the Southern market for Western stock,
bacon and grain gradually decreasing? Why do we hear
of hard times all over this broad and heretofore prosperous
land? Why can we not rally from a panic in a year, or by
the sale of one crop, as formerly? Echo answers why!
Where is the end of all this? When will we have better
times? Just when our national and State legislators will
see the importance of wise legislation and are willing to
give the necessary relief. But it is said that the already
enormous national debt is too great to be increased to the
extent required by the proposed act ; but let it be remembered that we propose to pay all the present and increased
debt in bonds, and that these bonds would be paid to the
people, who would use them to develop the country, and
improve the condition of the *entire* population, and the
increase of the population and wealth of the nation in the
next hundred years (the time allowed for their payment)
would be so enormously great the present and increased
national debt could be paid off in installments so easily that
neither the present or future generations *would ever* feel
it—yea, more! all direct taxation might be taken off the
people, and the public lands and custom house duties would
support the government and pay the entire debt within the
time prescribed. And let it be remembered that the interest on the proposed new debt, at three per cent. per
annum, would not exceed the interest we now pay on our
bonds, at from four to eight, and much of it in gold. Many
soldiers and citizens, if allowed, would take lands, instead
of bonds, for their claims, which would bring into cultivation the unused wealth of our vast Western domains.
Besides, a large national debt acts as ligaments, or bonds,
to hold a nation together, especially if the debt is due to

3

the people, instead of being held by foreigners. France, after losing a part of her territory, paid the immense war debt, due the Germans, in less than three years. And the Southern people have already paid, since the close of the war, into the public treasury of our nation more than the entire debt at the close of the war, which is, in addition to all other troubles brought on us, punishment enough for one generation. And now, in the name of all that is good, let us have relief from these heavy burdens. England and other nations carry large national debts, and none of them can do so as easily as we can, for our vast territory and growing wealth will enable us to do anything we wish, especially if our government be judiciously managed, and the people are relieved, as the proposed compromise would relieve them, as new life and energy would be imparted to all, old feelings of sectional animosity obliterated, and we would enter upon the life and duties of a new century in a manner as to insure peace, prosperity and happiness to the present and future generations of American citizens, as well as all those who would migrate to or from this great country. The emigration of the colored people to Africa, and the immigration of whites from Europe to America, would wake up the slumbering commerce and trade of the world, cheapen many articles of luxury and necessity. Let us, as a people, strive to hasten the happy period described in the sixtieth chapter of Isaiah, which says—"Violence shall no more be heard in the land, wasting nor destruction within thy borders; but thou shalt call thy walls Salvation, and thy gates Praise. The sun shall be no more thy light by day; neither for brightness shall the moon give light unto thee; but the Lord shall be unto thee an everlasting light, and thy God thy glory. Thy sun shall no more go down; neither shall thy moon withdraw itself; for the Lord shall be thine everlasting light, and the days of thy mourning shall be ended. Thy people also shall be all righteous;

they shall inherit the land forever, the branch of my planting, the work of my hands, that I may be glorified. A little one shall become a thousand, and a small one a strong nation : I the Lord will hasten it in His time." Doubtless the people of the Atlantic slope of this continent will be instruments of God of Christianizing Africa, and those of the Pacific slope of China. It is true the Constitution may have to be altered or amended to carry out this plan, but that may be done with as much propriety and justice as some of the amendments made during and since the war.

The future trade of Africa would pay our government handsomely for all she might judiciously expend in this way. England, France, Egypt, and other governments are making great efforts to secure the future trade of Africa. Will ours wait until the growing and important trade of Africa is divided and fully absorbed by the other great powers of the earth, or act in time to secure her proportionate part of it? From the following extract, taken from one of the letters of a lady correspondent of the *Baltimore Methodist*, from Philadelphia, the reader may have some faint idea of what the future trade of that vast and productive country would be :

"The Centennial exhibition is likely to open the eyes of our people to many good articles hitherto less thought of or generally unknown. Thus, in Agricultural Hall, the Liberia representation by Edward S. Morris & Co., draws great crowds. It covers much space, filled with samples of African produce, a globe with very large grains of Liberia coffee, which received the highest medal and diploma : ginger, indigo, arrow root, cam-wood, palm oil and soap made fresh under the trees at the Morris farm, Paul's river, Monrovia; cocoa, ivory, etc. Here is a robe worn by native chiefs; African mail bags, very small affairs; huge tusks of ivory ; a native African loom and shuttle, complete, weighing one pound and fourteen ounces, and specimens of unhulled coffee from Liberia and Brazil—the former twice as large in the grain as the latter. In 1871 Brazil exported 320,000,000 pounds. One thousand acres

are now under cultivation at Paul's river, the firm owning a
steamer which plies thither, fresh coffee being daily roasted,
and in much demand in the Exhibition.   The peculiar fea-
ture of the Liberia coffee is its greater strength and aroma.
It is sent all over the country in pound packages, so that it
can be tested.   When once tried, lovers of that excellent
thing, good coffee, will not fail to tell others of its value.
I thankfully acknowledge my indebtedness to a friend who
told me of it, and while passing the exhibit to-day, another,
to whom I had told my opinion, ordered fifty pounds."

A line of steamers running from each of our Atlantic
ports to Africa would secure that trade, carry the mails,
and convey our colored population to their fatherland as
fast as they might want to go.   An idea of this kind,
though on a smaller scale, was entertained by persons of
the Southern States prior to the war.   A memorial was presented to Congress in 1850, signed by Joseph Bryan, George
Nicholas Sanders, and others from Alabama and Georgia,
asking that body to establish a line of steamers from the
United States to the coast of Africa, " designed to promote
the colonization of free persons of color, to suppress the
African slave trade, to carry the mails, and to extend the
commerce of the United States," which report was referred
to a committee on Naval Affairs, and reported upon favorably in a report of 30 pages, signed by Fred. P. Stanton,
chairman, with an appendix added by the American Colonization Society, of 47 pages printed matter, showing the
great importance of such a plan to this country.   [See
" Report of Naval Committee on establishing a line of
Mail Steamers to the Western Coast of Africa," &c., dated
House of Representatives, Washington, August 1st, 1850.]

If such a proposition was of so much importance as to
be favorably reported on by a committee of one branch of
Congress in 1850, surely one like it, but more extensive,
would receive favorable consideration from both the great
bodies of Congress and the signature of the President now,
if asked for by the people.

NORTH AMERICA AND AFRICA. 21

A steamer leaving each of our Atlantic ports monthly, for Liberia, would carry out several thousand passengers annually and bring back large quantities of coffee, sugar, ivory, ginger, and many other tropical products, all of which would be greatly cheapened to us, give direct mail facilities to the Liberians and their friends here, and open up a new market for all our manufactured goods and implements in Liberia, whilst the withdrawal of our laborers would for a time enhance the value of our cotton, tobacco, &c., which would give new stimulus to our agriculture and pay us remunerative prices for our products. After their migration, these articles could be brought from Africa cheaper than to raise them here.

CHAPTER III.

Has African slavery in the United States been an injury or a benefit to that people? From a book called "Negroes in Negroland," a book of numerous quotations from various travelers in Africa, by H. R. Helper, a copy of which, with another volume, "Noon Day Exigencies in America," by the same author, kindly presented to the writer by Mr. Helper on his receiving a copy of the first edition of our little pamphlet, (and other works,) may be seen that slavery in all its barbaric hideousness existed from time immemorial in Africa, and though less manual labor was required of the slaves there than was required of the slaves in this country, their condition in Africa was infinitely worse than even in this country. There they were the subjects of all the tortures and miseries which idolatry and superstition could inflict; here they were brought under the influences of the Gospel and civilization: there they went without clothing, here they were clothed with New England goods;

there they wore neither hats nor shoes, here they wore both
made in Boston ; there they lived on roots, monkies, car-
rion, and the flesh of their own race, here they were fed
with corn and bacon from the West ; there their lives were
in the hands of witches and conjurers, here their lives were
protected by the laws of a Christian nation ; there they
knew nothing of the healing art and the hand of sympathy
and affection, here they were prescribed for when sick by
skilled physicians and nursed by cultivated persons. And
doubtless God, in his wisdom and goodness, suffered them
to be transferred to these shores in order that they might
learn to labor and to love, by being in contact with a race
already civilized.

And bondage seems to be God's peculiar instrument of
enlightening and redeeming, as well as afflicting nations
and people. Joseph was sold into bondage and imprisoned
in order that his father and brethren might be saved from
death when the impending famine should come, and the
Israelites were enslaved that they might find and enter the
promised land.

Thus it may be seen that all the sin of African slavery in
America is not chargeable to those who held slaves here
prior to their emancipation, but if sin it was, the responsi-
bility rests equally on all persons and nations who cap-
tured or brought and sold them to their late owners. The
doctrine of emancipation was growing, even among slave-
holders, and had politicians and outsiders kept hands off
the institution in the South would have gradually died
without the great struggle and damage received by both
races during and since the war waged for emancipation.
The war is over, but the bitter fruits are tasted yet by millions of our people ; both races have been injured by the
violence of the shock, and all of us must continue to feel
its sad results for scores of years to come, unless the hand
which struck the blow is stretched out to relieve. Mr.

Abraham Lincoln and many others who have occupied high positions in our government took grounds for gradual emancipation and indemnity for the owners of slaves, and the colonization of the free persons of color, by the general government. Had this been done immediately after the close of the war, times would now be better for us all.

Now, after eleven years of trial, hardship, poverty and suffering, which the Southern people of both races have borne, and are still bearing, and are also felt in all other sections of our common country, let the people arise in their might and magnanimity and say relief *shall be given* to *all* of *every* section in proportion to their losses and sufferings.

CHAPTER IV.

Is it best that the colored people of this country should go to their fathers' native land? Without arguing the subject, we will here introduce a letter written by Professor Thomas C. Upham, D. D., to the Rev. John Orcutt, D. D. Professor Upham was for more than forty years Professor of Mental and Moral Philosophy in Bowden College, Maine, and the popular author of several standard volumes:

NEW YORK, *April* 20, 1870.

REV. JOHN ORCUTT, D. D.

DEAR SIR:—Deprived by age and physical infirmity, of the privilege of taking a part in the more public efforts of the friends of African Colonization, I ask the favor, nevertheless, to express through you my continued interest, and my full and unquestioning faith in this noble and divine cause. My connection with the Colonization Society goes back some forty years; and from the beginning I have never doubted. In the darkest days, when the Society was assailed on every side, and not without some show of reason, my faith, looking beyond human errors to the wisdom of a controlling Providence, has remained unshaken.

Often in my solitary hours, not less than when pleading before God with my fellow-Christians for the restoration of erring humanity, have I seen and heard, in the depths of my spirit, the groans and the tears of suffering Africa. But I did not, and could not, at any period of my life, disconnect the interests of Africa from the interests of the negro race in this country. I did not remember Africa and forget the slave. In common with many others, I have felt deeply the great wrong of American slavery ; and my efforts, sympathy, and prayers have been with those who have labored for its termination. With me the two things have gone together. I have been unable to separate in my thoughts and in my deepest convictions the connection of the disenthralled and regenerated slave with the liberation of the land from which he came. But this connection, standing clear and firm in the convictions of many reflecting men, has not as yet found time to be fully realized. The slave is free, but Africa is not redeemed. The slave stands forth an American citizen, with the light of civilization and of Christianity, as well as of freedom thrown around him ; but the hundred and fifty millions of Africa are still almost universally in the bondage of ignorance, cruelty, and barbarous superstition. The means which were applicable to the restoration of other heathen lands and nations—the grand missionary work which has been carried on by the white race in other parts of the world—has been found in a great degree inapplicable here. So much so that many noble hearts have trembled before the difficulties of the problem, and have felt that human wisdom was not adequate to its solution.

But at this point of perplexity and darkness God unveils more clearly to our view the great plans which, amid clouds and shadows, and wrongs and sufferings, required the elaboration of centuries. A new power has arisen ; a nation has been born in a day ; and the heart and the eye of Africa are turned towards her own children ; and, with extended arms, and with more than the old Macedonian cry, she exclaims : " Come over and help us."

Some have supposed that this loud cry will be unheeded ; that the possession of new rights, or rather of old rights newly acknowledged, will so intoxicate and benumb the hearts of our colored brethren that they will not listen. I cannot believe it. I do not so understand the qualities of the negro race. The attributes which constitute their character are not justly estimated. When they shall have received, year after year, the instructions of colleges, we shall be able to pronounce more decisively upon the powers of their intellect. But intellectual traits alone do not constitute the whole of humanity. The colored race manifest a docility, a patience, a depth of feeling, a quickness of sympathy, a facility of religious belief, an appreciation of the kind, the good, and the joyous in life, which mark them as a people who have a higher work to do than to sit down in idleness.

It is very true that they will not go, and ought not to go, contrary to their own convictions. But on this point I have no anxiety. The great God who has watched over them from the beginning, who has marked their tears and heard their supplications, and in his own time has broken the chains of their bondage, will soon reveal to them the heights of their destiny, and will crown with a new glory the degradation which He has redeemed. It will not satisfy the African heart that the negro is recognized as a man, that he is an American citizen, that he has the right of suffrage, that he has a seat in the Senate; but with all the rights of an American, and educated in the best institutions of the country, he will find the God who has saved him opening his interior vision to behold the glory of being a co-worker in proclaiming the truths of freedom and justice, of civilization and Christianity throughout the length and breadth of Africa. Do not doubt it. Let the long-agitated question of the comparative mental position of the African race cease. A century hence, and perhaps much sooner, with the advantages of freedom and of equal education, the question will be settled on the philosophical basis of ascertained facts, and will be settled forever.

It is enough for us to know, in the light of the revelations which have become a part of history, that God is with the negro; and to know that the negro, no longer debased or restrained by slavery, will follow God's leading, whether his mission be here or elsewhere. Undoubtedly multitudes will stay here; America will be their home; both for their benefit and for our own. But other multitudes, touched with a higher aspiration and moulded to higher issues, will, in the course perhaps of a single century, reveal the African desert blossoming as the rose; and civilization and

4

Christianity flourishing under the protection of a system of republics, constituting under their own flag the United States of Africa.

In this great work, which constitutes a part of God's remedial system for the restoration of the world, colonization can now nobly lead. The way is now open for more energetic and widely-extended action, without the fears and doubts, and the liabilities to error, which have perplexed the past. And it cannot be doubted, that many influential men, who have heretofore stood aloof, are now ready for co-operation.

The day in which we live is remarkable for great and comprehensive plans. And these plans, so far as they originate in the great source of good, are not likely to fail. Let me say, therefore, that the hour has come. The men, the only class of men who are adequately fitted for the task, are ready. Let there be no want of means. Combine unity of purpose with unity of action; and let purpose and action go hand in hand with prayer and faith, which constitute the great elements of success.

With sentiments of most respectful and sincere regard,

I remain yours,

THOMAS C. UPHAM.

The Indians of this country have been moved from place to place at the expense of the government, and they are still being cared for (or exterminated as necessity demands) at a great annual cost. Do we not owe as much to the African race now among us? The Indians had a prior right to these lands on which we live, therefore we cannot easily make arrangements for their further removal; but the case is different with the African race: they have been torn from their native land by ruthless hands, backed by governmental authority, and should have the opportunity of going back at government expense, which they will embrace, gradually and surely, when they can see favorable arrangements are made for their safe and comfortable departure, and enough given them on arriving in their new homes to fit them for living above want. The Liberian government will give them enough land to support them,

on arriving; land far superior to any in this country, and
from which, two, three, and even four crops may be gather-
ed each year, and with less labor than one can be made
here. Many important facts, as to the temporal advantages they may secure by emigrating to Liberia, might be
copied in these pages from the "African Repository," a
very neat and valuable periodical issued quarterly by the
American Colonization Society, Colonization Rooms, No.
450 Pennsylvania Avenue, Washington, D. C., and other
important documents, kindly furnished the writer by Wm.
Coppinger, Esq., Corresponding Secretary of the African
Colonization Society, which kindness is hereby publicly
acknowledged and duly appreciated.

Mr. Coppinger will furnish the *Repository* to subscribers
at the low price of one dollar a year, and other information
gratuitously.

Judging from the history of missions in the past, we
must conclude that if the gospel is to penetrate and Christianize Africa, her own people, who have learned its saving
influences abroad, must be the successful missionaries. For
three hundred years Roman Catholics and Protestants have
been attempting to Christianize Africa by sending white
missionaries to labor there, but their signal failures prove
conclusively that the work must be done by another race;
and the unparalleled success of Liberia, shows the importance of all colored people of America taking steps in that
direction.

When the late and much lamented Southerner, Melville
B. Cox, was taking leave of his friends, as missionary for
Africa, his mother exclaimed: "Oh! Melville, Melville,
how can I give you up?" which, it is said, came near over-
powering the brave missionary; but God gave him strength
and words for the occasion, and he exclaimed: "Oh!
Africa, Africa, how can I give thee up?" And when he
died, his last words were, "Let a thousand missionaries

perish, ere Africa be given up." Let all colored ministers
and teachers, who feel as Melville Cox felt, take the lead
in this important matter, as did Moses and Aaron to lead
their people out of Egypt, through the wilderness, into the
promised land, and the multitude will follow.

CHAPTER V.

The sufferings of the Southern people of both races have,
within the past sixteen years, been beyond conception.
After a civil war of four years' duration, which taxed to
the utmost our energies, money and lives, contending with
ten to one on the field of battle, and the outside world
besides, with our ports closed, armies and supplies exhaust-
ed, we were compelled to surrender to the vast armies of
our brethren. Those victorious armies had consumed our
substance, laid waste our fields, burned our dwellings,
barns, gin-houses, cotton, tobacco, &c., as they marched
through our land; churches, graveyards, furniture, clothing, jewelry, plate, gold, silver, and valuable papers, were
desecrated, destroyed, or carried off, as best suited the feelings of men who were flushed with victory or inflamed by
passion or strong drink. Our system of labor being destroyed, money and credit gone, with sad hearts and empty
store-houses, we began life anew in April, 1865, to cultivate lands upon which was laid a heavy government tax,
and threatened with confiscation; compelled to rebuild our
houses and wasted fortunes with supplies from the North,
at fabulous prices, on credit or mortgages, with export duty
levied on our cotton, internal revenue on spirituous liquors
and tobacco, a licensed tax on many kinds of business, re-
construction acts and military governments following in
quick succession, carpet-baggers and thieves managing our
State governments in too many instances, Freedman's

Savings Banks victimized our colored population, and the National Banks, which were a monopoly, took all the interest they could get from our impoverished whites. All this, and more might be added, filled our poor-houses, asylums, grave-yards, jails and penitentiaries to overflowing, and produced a monetary panic which has lasted for three years, bids fair to last many more, and is being felt over the entire civilized world. And God's all-seeing eye can only penetrate the dark future, and tell what is to come of all this.

In order that persons who are not familiar with our sufferings, it may not be amiss to relate a few individual cases, among the hundred of thousands which have been endured by us. Two orphan brothers, who had been brought up in easy circumstances, married and entered active business life before they were twenty-one years of age, engaged heartily in all the internal improvements and benevolent enterprises within their reach for a quarter of a century : one of them filled the offices of post-master, justice of the peace and legislator for many years, lost, by the results of the war, nearly a hundred thousand dollars worth of property, and at the age of fifty-six, in midwinter and ill health, had to canvass his county on foot to sell books, in order to support a large family and prevent a Building and Loan Association from selling a home for which he had gone in debt. The other, and younger brother, lost over two hundred thousand dollars worth of valuable property, a splendid business, and his health; after giving up all that he had left of a fine estate, to pay debts which could not be paid during the war, retired from active city life to the country, with a dependent and helpless family, to battle with disease, poverty, and a selfish world, and for ten years he and his family have performed labor unsuited to their strength, deprived of former comforts, associates and friends, compelled to go in debt for a home, and his children failed to receive suitable educations for want of the means to pro-

vide them. Two grandfathers of these brothers were soldiers in the revolutionary war of 1776, which gained our
independence as a nation. One of them served seven years,
and was in most of the important battles north of the
Potomac, and was one of the picked hundred men who took
Stony Point with empty guns, at the point of the bayonet.
The other served five years hard service. Neither of those
old soldiers, or any of their posterity, ever applied for or
received one dollar of the pension money due them from
the United States government, and their posterity lost by
the late civil war over a million and a half dollars worth
of property. A young lady had been at school and teach-
ing in Western North Carolina during the war. At its
close, she started alone for her home in western Georgia,
met with an aged minister, and traveled with him in a
wagon two hundred miles in the wake of Sherman's devastating track, amid the ruins of valuable plantations, lost fortunes, destroyed homes, and the blackened, solitary chimneys which could not burn, to find her parents and many
other loved ones, who had never known want, in need of
shelter, food and raiment.

An aged minister of a large and influential denomina-
tion of Christians, who had devoted his life to his work,
was so reduced by the war, that he sat down on his door-
step to eat his meals of dry corn bread, and walked from
house to house, and from church to church, to visit and
preach to his people. Many others did like service until better fare and other horses could be had. Many aged, infirm or
helpless persons were deprived of food, clothing and shelter in a day or night—want and suffering took the places
of comfort and plenty almost everywhere in our once fair
and happy land.

A one-armed Confederate soldier has, for years, support-
ed his family by mortgaging his horse, wagon and growing
crops, and working rented land. On settling with a mer-

cantile firm who had supplied the pressing wants of his
family for two years, gave up his wagon, horse and crop to
pay out, and carried his gears off on his shoulder, walking
to his new home, to go in debt again for another blind
horse to work more rented land, holding the plow with one
hand, while ploughing for another crop, while his family
are to live by the aid of others or suffer.

An aged and highly respected physician, who had been
compelled to quit his profession in early life, because of a
fall from a vehicle which made him a cripple for life, after
the war took to mending old shoes for his bread. Many of
the sick, and some in very *critical* conditions, were carried out of their comfortable rooms and laid in the streets
or roads, while their homes were being burned; others
were compelled to live for a time on parched corn, picked
up after the army horses had trodden it under their feet.

To prove our statements not to be overdrawn, we here
copy from a Western paper accounts of General Sheridan's
mode of warfare in Virginia, and General Sherman's march
to the sea, written by their own men:

WHAT MIGHT HAVE BEEN.

We propose to show what soldiers will do when their
respective governments pretend to absolve them from all
obligations to obey God, and place them under the command
of men, whose word is law and whose trade is slaughter.
And as the scenes of horror and devastation during the
rebellion, were so much more numerous and heart-rending
at the South than at the North, from the fact that the
former was the seat of war, we shall present facts from that
region, though to some extent in the language of our own
men.

After the battle of Fisher's Hill, in Virginia, General
Sheridan wrote from Strasburg as follows: "Lieut. J. R.
Meigs, my engineer officer, was murdered beyond Harris-
burg, near Dayton. For this atrocious act, all the houses
within an area of five miles were burned. In moving back
to this point, the whole country, from the Blue Ridge to

the North Mountain, has been made entirely untenable for
a rebel army. I have destroyed over two thousand barns,
filled with wheat and hay and farming implements; over
seventy mills filled with flour and wheat; have driven in
front of the army over four thousand head of stock, and
have killed and issued to the troops, not less than three
thousand sheep. This destruction embraces the Luray valley and the Little Fork valley, as well as the main valley."

A Northern correspondent who traveled with Sherman's
army during its march to the sea, thus reports its prowess
in pillage: "Such little freaks as taking the last chicken,
the last pound of meal, the last bit of bacon, and the only
remaining scraggy cow, from a poor woman and her flock
of children, black or white not considered, came under the
order of legitimate business. Even crockery, bed covering,
and clothes were fair spoils. As for plate or jewelry or
watches, these were things rebels had no use for. Men with
pockets plethoric with silver and gold coin; soldiers sink-
ing under the weight of plate and fine bedding materials;
lean mules and horses, with the richest trappings of Brus-
sels carpets, and hangings of fine chenille, negro wenches,
particularly good looking ones, decked in satin and silks,
and sporting diamond ornaments, officers with sparkling
rings, that would set Tiffany in raptures, gave color to the
stories of hanging up or fleshing an ' old cuss' to make him
shell out. A planter's house was overrun in a jiffy; boxes,
drawers and escritories were ransacked with a landable zeal,
and emptied of their contents. If the spoils were ample,
the depredators were satisfied, and went off in peace; if
not, everything was torn and destroyed, and most likely
the owner was tickled with sharp bayonets into a confes-
sion where he had his treasures hid. If he escaped and
was hiding in a thicket, this was *prima facie* evidence that
he was a skulking rebel; and most likely some ruffian, in
his zeal to get rid of such vipers, gave him a dose of lead,
which cured him of his Secesh tendencies. Sorghum bar-
rels were knocked open, bee hives rifled, while their angry
swarms rushed frantically about. Indeed, I have seen a
soldier knock a planter down because a bee stung him.
Should the house be deserted, the furniture is smashed in
pieces, music is pounded out of four hundred dollar pianos
with the ends of muskets. Mirrors were wonderfully multiplied, and rich cushions and carpets carried off to adorn

teams and war steeds. After all was cleared out, most likely some set of stragglers wanted to enjoy a good fire, and set the house, debris of furniture, and all the surroundings in a blaze. This is the way Sherman's army lived on the country."

In the language of a historian of the war, we report other scenes as follows : " Gen. Sherman was the author of the sentiment, 'War is cruelty and you cannot refine it.' This extraordinary doctrine he at once proceeded to put in practice by depopulating Atlanta, and driving from their homes thousands of helpless women and children. It was the most cruel and savage act of the war. In vain the Mayor of Atlanta had pointed out to him that the country south of the city was crowded already with refugees, and without houses to accommodate the people, and that many had no other shelter but what they might find in churches and out buildings, that the consequences would be woe, horror and suffering, which could not be described by words. Sherman was inexorable. He affected the belief that Atlanta might again be rendered formidable in the hands of the Confederates, and resolved, in his own words, " to wipe it out." The old and decrepit ones were hunted from their homes, they were packed into railroad cars; tottering old age and helpless youth were crowded together; wagons were filled with wrecks of household goods, and the trains having deposited their medley freight at Rough and Ready, the exiles were then left to shift for themselves. On the night of the 15th, the torch was applied to Atlanta, and when the merciless commander had already created a solitude, he determined to make a second conflagration, by the light of which his marching columns might commence their journey to the sea. The work was done with terrible completeness ; buildings covering two hundred acres were in flames at one time ; the heavens were an expanse of livid fire ; and amid the wild and terrific scene, the Federal bands played " John Brown's soul goes marching on." The next morning, Sherman's army moved from a scene of desolation such as had occurred in no modern picture of civilized war. From four to five thousand houses were reduced to ruins ; and four hundred left standing was the melancholy remnant of Atlanta. Nearly all the shade trees in the park and city had been destroyed, and the suburbs, stripped of

5

timber, presented to the eye one vast, naked, ruined, deserted camp.

After Sherman had taken Savannah, he wrote in his official report, as follows: "We have consumed the corn and fodder in the region of country thirty miles on either side of a line from Atlanta to Savannah, as also the sweet potatoes, cattle, hogs, sheep and poultry, and have carried away more than ten thousand horses and mules, as well as a countless number of their slaves. I estimate the damage done to the State of Georgia and its military resources at one hundred millions of dollars, at least twenty millions of which has inured to our advantage, and the remainder is simple waste and destruction."

From Savannah, Sherman invaded South Carolina, where his track of destruction is thus described: "The country was converted into one vast bonfire. The pine forests were fired, the rosin factories were fired, the public buildings and private dwellings were fired. The middle of the finest day looked black and gloomy, for a dense smoke arose on all sides, clouding the very heavens. At night the tall pine trees seemed so many pillars of fire. The scenes of license and plunder which attended these conflagrations, were even more terrible. Long trains of fugitives lined the roads, with women and children, and horses and stock and cattle, seeking refuge from the pursuers. Long lines of wagons covered the highways. Half-naked people cowered from the winter under bush-tents in the thickets, under the eaves of houses, under the railroad sheds, and in old cars left them along the route. Habitation, village after village, sent up its signal flames to the others, and lighted the sky with crimson horrors. Granaries were emptied, and where the grain was not carried off, it was strewn to waste under the feet of the cavalry, or consigned to the fire which consumed the dwelling. The roads were covered with butchered cattle, hogs, mules and the costliest furniture. Valuable cabinets, rich pianos, were not only hewn to pieces, but bottles of ink, turpentine, oil, whatever could efface or destroy, was employed to defile or ruin. Horses were ridden into the houses. Beautiful homesteads of the parish gentry, with their wonderful tropical gardens, were ruined. Ancient dwellings of black cypress, one hundred years old, were given to the torch as recklessly as were the rude hovels Choice pictures and works of art from Europe, select and numerous libraries, objects of peace wholly, were destroyed. The inhabitants were left to starve, compelled to feed only upon the garbage to be found in the abandoned camps of the soldiers. The corn scraped up from the spots where the horses fed, was the only means of life left to thousands lately in affluence."

Columbia was surrendered to Sherman on the morning of the 17th of February, by the Mayor, Mr. Goodwin, who asked for the citizens " the treatment accorded by the usages of civilized warfare." Sherman promised this. But the work of pillage had begun when the Federal troops had first reached the head of Main street. Stores were broken open, and the contents strewn on the sidewalk ; citizens were robbed in the street; no one felt safe in his own dwelling. Robbery was going on at every corner. Meanwhile, the flames spread from side to side, from front to rear, from street to street. All the thoroughfares were quickly crowded with helpless women and children, some in their night clothes. Agonized mothers seeking their children, all affrighted and terrified, were rushing on all sides from the raging flames and falling houses. Invalids had to be dragged from their beds, and lay exposed to the flames and smoke that swept the streets, or to the cold of the open air in the back yards. The sun rose with a wan countenance, peering dimly through the dense vapor which seemed wholly to overspread the firmament. The best and most beautiful portions of Columbia lay in ruins. Eighty-four squares of buildings had been destroyed, with scarcely the exception of a single house. The capitol building, six churches, eleven banking establishments, the schools of learning, the shops of art and trade, of invention and manufacture, shrines equally of religion, benevolence and industry, were all buried together in one congregated ruin. Nothing remained but the tall, specter-looking chimneys. The noble looking trees that shaded the streets, the flower gardens that graced them, were blasted and withered by fire. On every side there were ruins and smoking masses of blackened walls, and between, in desolate groups, reclining on mattress, or bed, or earth, were wretched women and children, gazing vacantly on the site of what had been their home.

" The burning of Columbia was but of a piece with Sherman's record. He had burned six out of every seven farm

houses on the route of his march.   Before he reached Columbia, he had burned Blackville, Graham, Bamberg, Bu-
ford's Bridge, Lexington, and had not spared the humblest
hamlet.   After he left Columbia, he gave to the flames the
villages of Allston, Pomaria, Winnsboro, Blackstock, Society Hill, and the towns of Camden and Cheraw."

Reader, this is war, and this is what war makes of men
who were once tender-hearted and humane.   We do not
quote these descriptions to condemn Northern soldiers, but
to condemn war itself.   We have before intimated, that if
the North had been the theatre of the war, and the Southern armies the invaders, they would have done no better,
and we of the North should have more vivid impressions of
its dreadful consequences than we now have.—*The Informer, Elgin, Ill.*

The editor of the *Informer* says, " Reader, this is war,
* * * that if the North had been the theater of the war,
and the Southern armies the invaders, they would have
done no better, and we of the North should have more
vivid impressions of its dreadful consequences than we now
have."

Did not Southern armies invade Northern territory
during the war?   Did they act thus?   Did the British
armies of 1776–'82, as they traversed these then colonies,
fighting to conquer real rebels, leave such devastation be-
hind them?   Let history tell the tale.   The object of the
writer of this humble volume, is not to open the wounds
made by the civil strife.   God forbid that these slowly
healing wounds should ever be re-opened, but that they
should continue to heal, until the last vestige of a scar shall
disappear forever.   But the easiest and best way to heal
them, is to compensate those who lost so much in the conflict, give back to the fallen, the weak, the oppressed of
every color, class and section, their homes, their equal
rights, their heritage for which our ancestors suffered, bled
and died.

The blood, limbs, lives, tears and sighs shed in the late unfortunate strife cannot be given back, but as far as possible let justice be done to all, that peace, harmony and prosperity shall once more be enjoyed by *all* our people.

CHAPTER VI.

The colored population of the South have suffered intensely since the war; persuaded, as they were, to leave their old homes, they have wandered in exile from one part of the nation to another, in search of comforts and luxuries they have not found—not even " the forty acres of land and a mule"—thousands upon thousands of them have sickened and died, having no kind, sympathizing hand to administer to their wants. Around every city and town their newly made graves are numbered by the thousand, and covering land by the acre. During the year 1865, as many as fifty to seventy-five of them died a day in the city of Newbern, N. C., with small pox. Ten thousand fell there in a single year, or at least that was the estimate made by those who lived there, one of whom was the writer. In various other ways have we of both races suffered. One hundred millions of dollars of our scanty funds have gone into Northern Insurance Companies, which have not, and most of it will never return, as many policies have been forfeited for want of funds to keep them up. Other millions of dollars have gone to the city of " Brotherly Love," during our Centennial. Are its people willing that we shall be put upon our feet again?

Northern merchants and manufacturers are constantly receiving the earnings of our united labor. One of our honored sons, in a speech made to a large crowd in Central Park in New York, after the nomination of Messrs. Seymonr and Blair for the offices of President and Vice President, said: "Let us go home and elect our candidates, and we of the South will send our rich products here and lay them down upon your wharves, and exchange them for your *Fragrant Sozodont* and *Radway's Ready Relief.*"

Messrs. Seymour and Blair were not elected, but we have sent all our cotton, tobacco, naval stores, etc., on as fast as we have been able to produce them, and taken in exchange many articles of less value.

The main question in this whole matter is, Can the United States government undertake so great a task as this, with her present national debt, without oppressing the already impoverished and depressed people? We answer, *Yes!* All of our present population would obtain relief thereby, either directly or indirectly. The payment of the present and the increased debt, though large, could be postponed until the country recuperated, when our increased population and wealth would enable us to pay it, and more, if needed, in annual, or five or ten yearly installments; and the interest, if at three per cent., might be paid annually in gold; and with our vast West and South filled up with people of means and energy from the North and Europe, with lines of steamers constantly coming into our ports from Europe, Africa, and other countries, we could pay off the bonds of the government in gold received at the ports, as they would fall due, without a single dollar from internal revenue, or any other direct tax ever being laid upon this or future generations of our people, if we kept out of war, which we should strive to do, and settle all internal or foreign difficulties by arbitration instead of resorting to arms, as has been our custom.

Slavery with us is dead forever, and we of the South would not have it back if we could; we have suffered too much by it. Clear of it and the responsibilities which attended it, we would not resume them, but we would have, if we could, the restitution made to us which justice, equity and common law, as well as fraternal feeling ought to give us; and the colored people, if they will accept a part of it in the way proposed, they should have at least one-third of their former value expended for the future good of them and their race.

Our families who have been accustomed to the services of the colored people, think they could not well do without them, and farmers may be of the same opinion, but let it be remembered that their removal could only be a very gradual arrangement. Our cooking and washing now done by hand in each house, could and would be done by co-operative companies, and by steam and machinery, and our farms be converted into stock and grass farms, and culti vated with improved machinery, while surplus lands could be made to produce timber which will be greatly needed and very profitable ere long. The raising of timber, beef, mutton, pork, and many other articles for other countries, which could be produced more easily than our present money crops, would gradually be taken hold of by us, and we would gradually accommodate ourselves to a new and better mode of living. The same may be said of the trade or patronage of our colored people, i. e. other trade, service and patronage would be gradually introduced and substi tuted for theirs, which, in the end, would be more remu nerative and satisfactory. Now, if these arguments are not overdrawn, and the writer believes they are only very im perfectly presented, it is the interest and duty of every citi zen, of every State, of both *races*, to sign a memorial to Congress, asking the passage of a law at once by which this great plan of compromise and relief may be given to our entire people, in order that peace, prosperity, good will and happiness be restored to all of both races in our once pros perous, but now impoverished country; and we would see persons who were made bankrupts by the war, hunting up

old debts, which were debarred from collection, paid up.
new ones quickly settled, old homes beautified, our waste
places made to bloom as the flower gardens of our once
happy wives bloomed, and such a flood-tide of prosperity
and good feeling set in as to cause a new era to dawn upon
us as a people; we would pay our entire national debt in
the century following, learn war no more, and be instru-
mental in the hands of God in evangelizing the world, and
our posterity could celebrate the next Centennial of American Independence without the grim monster, poverty,
staring us in the face (as now), sectional bickerings or feelings of hate to mar their happiness.   This compromise will
bury forever, all idea of repudiation, and our people will be
able to inculcate into the minds of our children the importance of promptly meeting all personal, State and National
obligations.

Let us go at this work promptly, earnestly and honestly,
that it may be as a monument of truth and justice erected
in the hearts of our children to remind them of the importance of *national honor, peace and good will.*

Let both the great political parties take hold of it, and
have an equal share of the glories arising therefrom; let it
be a national and not a sectional or partizan work, that it
may heal *forever* all the old issues of the past, and give a
glow of good feeling to our future.

It is said "our Northern brethren will never consent to
such a compromise." Why not? They may restore, by
this act, their own as well as our former prosperity, prevent
repudiation of some of our State or National debts, divert
much suffering in this and other countries, and harmonize
many discordant elements.

In conclusion, the reader is requested to read the instructions given by the God of heaven and earth to the children
of Israel, found in the 19th chapter of Leviticus.

That co-operative action be had in this matter, a form of a memorial to Congress is appended to these pages. Let every one who feels an interest in the great work, copy and obtain the signatures of his neighbors to it, and enclose it to one of our Senators or Representatives in Congress as early as practicable, and urge its adoption.

FORM OF A MEMORIAL TO CONGRESS.

STATE OF —————————,

County of————, ————, 187

To the Honorable Senators and Members of the House of Representatives of the United States in Congress assembled:

We, the citizens of the United States, most respectfully petition your honorable bodies to enact a law by which all citizens of every section of the United States may be paid for all their property destroyed for them by the governments and armies of *both sides* during the late war between the States, in bonds bearing three per cent. interest per annum, maturing within the next hundred years.

And we also petition that all soldiers, or their legal representatives, of *both* armies and every section, be paid in bonds or *public lands* for their lost time, limbs and lives, while engaged in the late unfortunate civil conflict, and we will ever pray, &c.

www.ingramcontent.com/pod-product-compliance
Lightning Source LLC
Chambersburg PA
CBHW021549270326
41930CB00008B/1430